20 FUN FACTS ABOUT STICK BUGS

By Heather Moore Niver

Please visit our website, www.garethstevens.com. For a free color catalog of all our high-quality books, call toll free 1-800-542-2595 or fax 1-877-542-2596.

Publisher Cataloging Data

Niver, Heather Moore
    20 fun facts about stick bugs / by Heather Moore Niver.
         p.   cm. – (Fun fact file. Bugs!)
    Includes bibliographical references and index.
    Summary: This book describes stick bugs, including their physical characteristics, eating habits, and how they reproduce.
    Contents: Cool creepy crawlers – From basic brown to wild wings – Come out and play, stick bug – The longest insect in the world – What's that awful smell? – Girls rule! – Extraordinary eggs – Stick bug babies – Munch time! – Weird and wonderful.
    ISBN 978-1-4339-8251-4 (hard bound) – ISBN 978-1-4339-8252-1 (pbk.)
ISBN 978-1-4339-8253-8 (6-pack)
    1. Stick insects—Juvenile literature   [1. Stick insects]   I. Title
        2013
    595.7/29—dc23

First Edition

Published in 2013 by
Gareth Stevens Publishing
111 East 14th Street, Suite 349
New York, NY 10003

Designer: Sarah Liddell
Editor: Greg Roza

Photo credits: Cover, p. 1 David Barrie/Flickr/Getty Images; p. 5 Gregory MD./PhotoResearchers/Getty Images; pp. 6, 20, 21 Eric Isselee/Shutterstock.com;
p. 7 Jason Edwards/National Geographic/Getty Images; p. 8 kurt_G/Shutterstock.com;
p. 9 Hemera Technologies/PhotoObjects.net/Thinkstock.com; p. 10 David W. Leindecker/Shutterstock.com; pp. 11, 14, 25 Dr. Morley Read/Shutterstock.com; p. 12 Fletcher and Baylis -/Photo Researchers/Getty Images; p. 13 iStockphoto/Thinkstock.com;
p. 15 Tim Laman/National Geographic/Getty Images; p. 16 © iStockphoto.com/preflight;
p. 18 BIOPHOTO ASSOCIATES/Photo Researchers/Getty Images; p. 19 rck_953/Shutterstock.com; p. 22 Visuals Unlimited, Inc./Mark Plonsky/Visuals Unlimited/Getty Images; p. 23 Aminart/Oxford Scientific/Getty Images; p. 24 © iStockphoto.com/GlobalP;
p. 26 © iStockphoto.com/nik04; p. 27 Paul Bertner/Flickr Open/Getty Images;
p. 29 Karen Moskowitz/axi/Getty Images.

Printed in the United States of America

CPSIA compliance information: Batch #CW13GS: For further information contact Gareth Stevens, New York, New York at 1-800-542-2595.

Contents

Words in the glossary appear in **bold** type the first time they are used in the text.

Cool Creepy Crawlers

Is that stick moving all by itself? Look again. You just might have a stick bug in your yard. Stick bugs are sometimes called stick insects or walking sticks. These creepers look like plant parts, which helps **camouflage** them so they can hide from **predators**.

Stick bugs and leaf insects are both part of the order, or group, called phasmids (FAZ-muhdz). Scientists have spotted more than 3,000 different kinds of stick bugs. They discover more stick bugs every year.

stick bug

The word "phasmid" is Greek for "apparition," or "ghost," which describes this hard-to-see bug pretty well.

A stick bug isn't just a stick. Like other insects, its body has three different parts.

Stick bug bodies have three parts. The head contains its brain and mouth. Three pairs of legs are attached to its thorax. So are wings if the stick bug has them. The stick bug's abdomen holds several **organs**, such as its stomach.

The Indian stick bug, shown here, is also known as the laboratory stick insect because scientists like to study it.

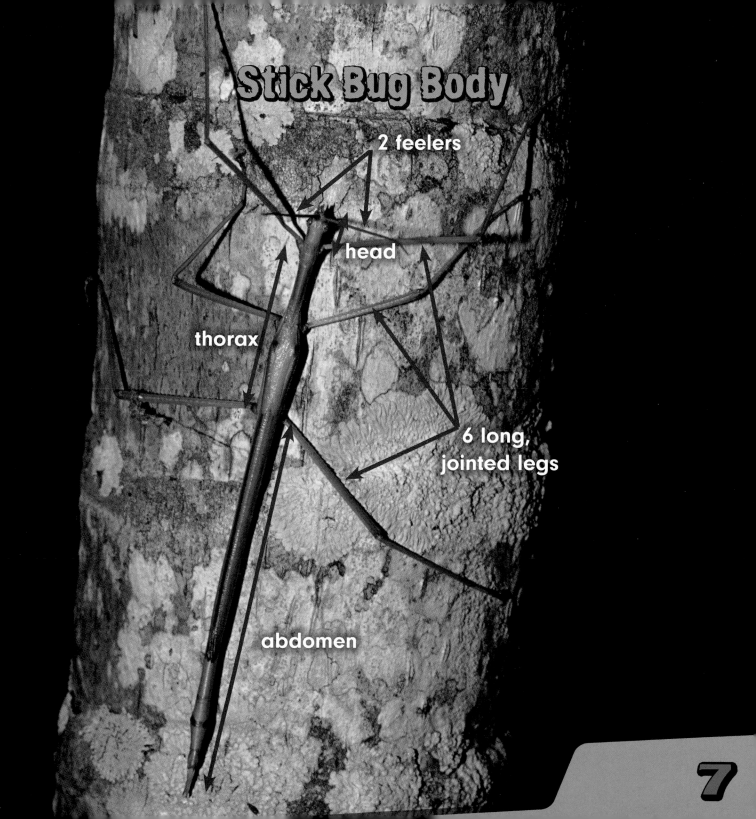

Stick Bug Body

2 feelers

head

thorax

6 long, jointed legs

abdomen

FACT 2

Stick bugs sometimes have crazy colors and patterns on their bodies.

Many stick bugs are brown. This helps them hide in trees. However, stick bugs come in many other colors. They can also be green, black, gray, or even blue. These colors help them hide against moss, leaves, and even flowers.

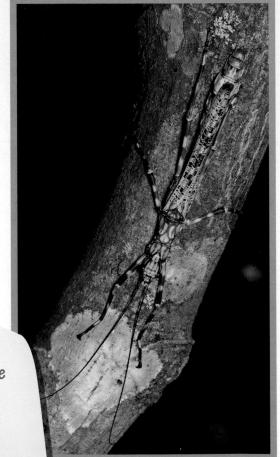

Some stick bugs look just like moss or tree bark.

Some stick bugs use their colorful wings to fool predators.

Some stick bugs have bright wings they show when a predator is nearby. Then, the stick bug quickly drops to the ground and hides its wings. The predator looks all over for the bright wings while the stick bug hides among leaves and sticks.

Come Out and Play, Stick Bug

FACT 4

Stick bugs are great at hiding, but they aren't shy.

Stick bugs can hide in sticks and leaves, but most of them hang out in the open. They stay so still that they're unlikely to be noticed. When they move, stick bugs sway, or slowly move back and forth, to make it look like they're a stick blowing in the breeze.

Keep an eye out for stick bugs, because one might be right under your nose.

Stick bugs stay up all night long.

You're most likely to see a stick bug at night. That's because they're nocturnal animals, meaning they're most active at night. During the day, they hide under leaves and plants to avoid becoming a meal.

The Longest Insect in the World

The biggest stick bug is almost 2 feet (61 cm) long.

The littlest walking sticks are about 0.5 inch (1.3 cm) long. Not all stick bugs are small. The biggest walking sticks are close to 13 inches (33 cm) long. When they stretch out their legs, they can reach 21 inches (53 cm)!

The biggest stick bug of all is the Borneo stick bug, or Chan's megastick.

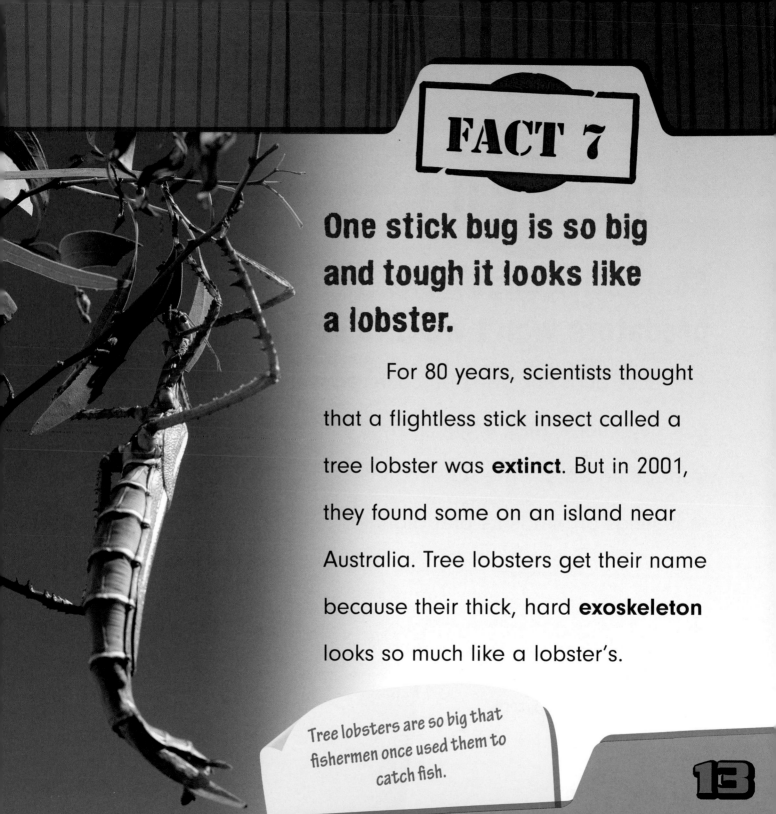

One stick bug is so big and tough it looks like a lobster.

For 80 years, scientists thought that a flightless stick insect called a tree lobster was **extinct**. But in 2001, they found some on an island near Australia. Tree lobsters get their name because their thick, hard **exoskeleton** looks so much like a lobster's.

Tree lobsters are so big that fishermen once used them to catch fish.

FACT 8

Some stick bugs make themselves stink so predators won't want to eat them.

Stick bugs shouldn't be confused with stinkbugs, but some can get smelly. They might spray a stinky brown liquid to keep from being eaten. The American walking stick can squirt a fluid that stings or blinds its predators for a while.

The spiny devil walking stick sprays a nasty brownish liquid to scare off predators.

FACT 9

Stick bugs sometimes lose legs to escape a predator.

Stick bugs have an interesting way of avoiding hungry mice, birds, reptiles, spiders, and bats. If a young stick bug is in danger, it can drop off one of its legs to escape a hungry predator. It can grow the leg back the next time it **molts**.

You can see the sharp spines on the back leg of this stick bug.

FACT 10

Some stick bugs know how to play dead.

Some walking sticks pretend to be dead in hopes that a hungry predator will pass them by. Others have sharp spines on their legs. When they're in danger, the stick bug can stab at the enemy.

Super Stick Bugs

common name	funky features
Indian stick insect	dark brown to bright green color
pink-wing stick insect	light brown with bright pink wings
thorny stick insect	fast moving with thorns on its back
titan stick insect	longest stick bug in Australia
spur-legged phasmid	males have wings, but females don't
Lord Howe Island stick insect	also called tree lobster because of its thick shell
goliath stick insect	green with yellow spots; green wings with red marks
big-headed stick insect	large head; small wings but doesn't fly
crown stick insect	lumps on its head look like a crown
peppermint stick insect	named for its minty smell

Girls Rule!

FACT 11

A female stick bug doesn't need a male to have babies.

Female stick bugs might be some of the most independent women on the planet. They can have babies without the help of a male walking stick. This is called parthenogenesis (pahr-thuh-noh-JEH-nuh-suhs). They lay eggs that **hatch** into clones, or exact copies of themselves.

These are the eggs of an Indian stick bug.

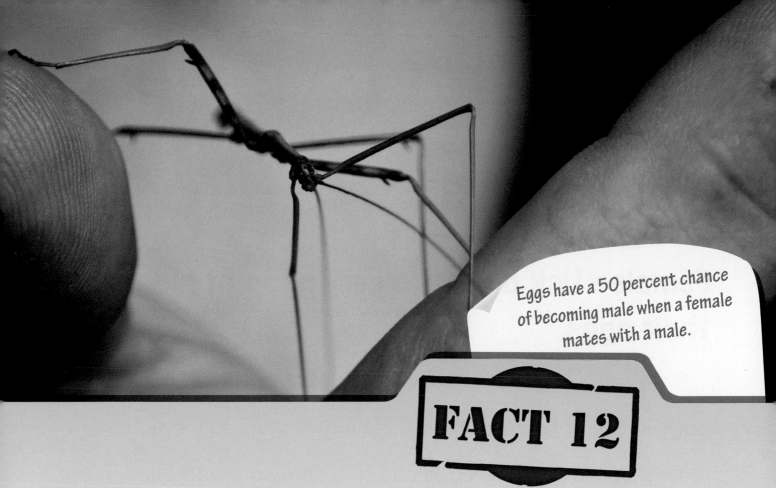

Eggs have a 50 percent chance of becoming male when a female mates with a male.

FACT 12

There are a lot more girls than boys in the stick bug world.

Stick bug mothers can **mate** with a male if they want to. This is the only time there's a chance that an egg will hatch a male. Female stick bugs are usually bigger than males.

Extraordinary Eggs

Female stick bugs are very good at hiding their eggs.

To keep eggs safe, many female stick bugs hide their eggs in soil or hollow plants. Others glue them to the bottom of leaves. Some drop the eggs one at a time so predators don't find a large cluster of eggs to dine on.

Stick bug eggs come in many different shapes depending on the type of stick bug that lays them.

Some kinds of stick bugs want ants to steal their eggs.

Some stick bug **species** lay eggs with a special bump that ants like to snack on. The ants bring the eggs to their nest, eat the bump, and leave the rest. The eggs stay in their nest, safe from predators, until they hatch.

capitulum (bump)

Stick Bug Babies

FACT 15

Baby walking sticks look like tiny copies of adult walking sticks.

Many newborn insects look like worms and then change to look like their parents as they grow. Not stick bugs. When a baby stick bug, called a nymph, breaks out of its egg, it looks just like its mother—except a lot smaller.

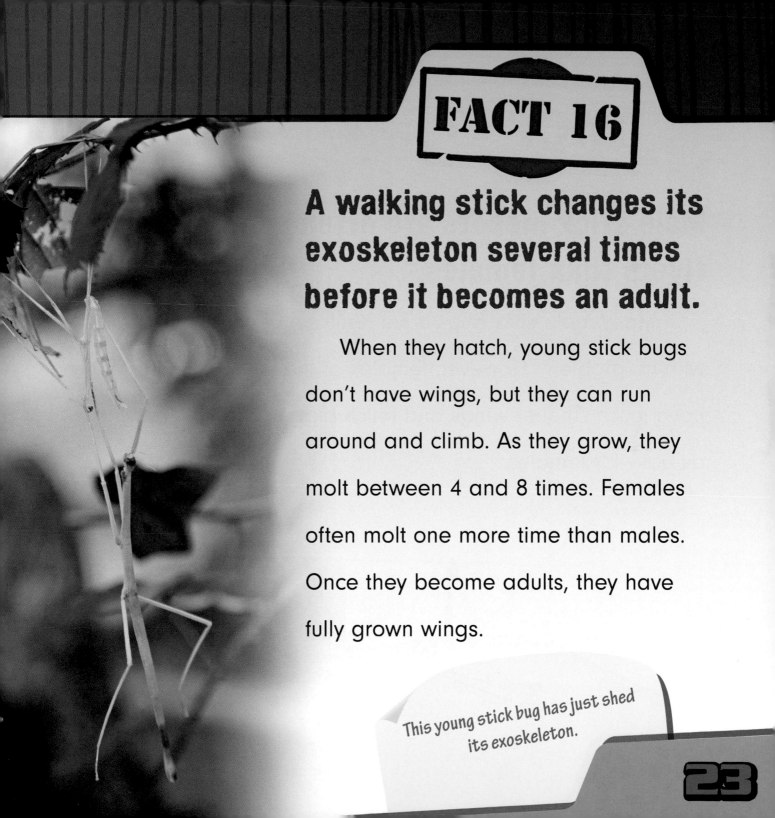

A walking stick changes its exoskeleton several times before it becomes an adult.

When they hatch, young stick bugs don't have wings, but they can run around and climb. As they grow, they molt between 4 and 8 times. Females often molt one more time than males. Once they become adults, they have fully grown wings.

This young stick bug has just shed its exoskeleton.

FACT 17

Male stick insects are often much better flyers than females.

Many male stick bugs have a full set of wings and can fly with no problem. However, females of the same species often have much smaller wings and much bigger bodies. So flying isn't as easy for females.

Some females don't have wings, and not all species have wings.

Munch Time!

Stick bugs munch on leaves for lunch.

Stick bugs usually live in warm areas, but some live in cooler parts of the planet, too. They like to live in forests and grasslands, which are full of the tasty leaves they like to eat. Walking sticks are herbivores, which means they only eat plants.

This stick bug is eating the skin it recently shed.

FACT 19

Sometimes stick bugs eat their own skin.

After a young stick bug molts, it might eat its old skin. It sounds gross, but this is a great way for the bugs to get healthy **nutrients**. By eating their skin, walking sticks also hide a sign of where they are from predators.

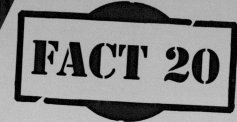

Other bugs chow down on stick bug poop.

Stick bugs help feed smaller insects in a really weird way. They use their strong mouthparts, called mandibles, to chew and break down plant leaves. Their droppings contain plant material that other smaller insects feed on.

Weird and Wonderful

Stick bugs are strange, slow-moving insects. They may not be fast, but they'll probably beat you in a game of hide-and-seek. Few animals hide as well as a stick bug.

Stick bugs are some cool creepy crawlers you might want to check out. Some people even keep them as pets. However, if too many are removed from their natural homes as pets, the bugs could become extinct. We want these cool critters to live a long time!

Stick bugs are easy to take care of.

Glossary

camouflage: colors or shapes in animals that allow them to blend with their surroundings

exoskeleton: the hard outer covering of an animal's body

extinct: no longer living

hatch: to break open or come out of

mate: to come together to make babies

molt: the act of shedding an exoskeleton that has become too small

nutrient: something a living thing needs to grow and stay alive

organ: a part inside an animal's body

predator: an animal that hunts other animals for food

species: a group of plants or animals that are all of the same kind

For More Information

Books

Hartley, Karen, Chris Macro, and Philip Taylor. *Stick Insect.* Chicago, IL: Heinemann Library, 2008.

Markle, Sandra. *Stick Insects: Masters of Defense.* Minneapolis, MN: Lerner Publications, 2008.

Petrie, Kristin. *Walking Sticks.* Edina, MN: ABDO Publishing, 2009.

Websites

Australian Stick Insects

www.ozanimals.com/wildlife/Insect/Stick-Insects.html
Learn more about the stick bugs of Australia with photos and details about many different kinds.

Care of Stick Insects

australianmuseum.net.au/Care-of-Stick-Insects
This is a great site to learn more about walking sticks with photos, facts, and maps.

Index